Wondrous Creatures

Explore a World of Animals from A to Z

To: Kai, Animals are awesome!

Dean Jacobs 5-14-12

World travels, writing, and photography by
Dean Jacobs

Educational text co-authored by
Amy Tharp

ISBN 978-0-9749441-1-1
Printed in United States of America

Wondrous Creatures I Found

by

_____

Print your name on the line.

The world begins at your door

Even your yard is part of an amazing world that is filled with **Wondrous Creatures**.
So let's start finding some of them, wherever you are!
See how many mammals, amphibians, birds, fish, and reptiles you can find.
Write the name of the animal in the left column and where you found it in the right column.
Draw stars ★ next to your favorite creatures!

_____   _____

_____   _____

_____   _____

_____   _____

_____   _____

_____   _____

_____   _____

_____   _____

_____   _____

Dedications

To my brother, Dale Jacobs, who seems to always be there when I need him. And to all who smile whenever they see an animal.
- Dean Jacobs

To the students and staff at Highland Elementary. And to my sons, Connor and Garrett, of course.
-Amy Tharp

Acknowledgments

The process of creating a book takes many steps and is a journey in itself. There are many to recognize. The idea for this book was born over time and started when my friend Mary Boul, an elementary teacher in Iowa, kept requesting photos of animals for class projects. She suggested an animal book for students.

I want the book to be a tool to inspire and educate. I wish to thank Amy Tharp, a passionate elementary teacher in Colorado, who suggested adding important educational information. She compiled research and did a masterful job of crafting it into language for children. This gives the book real educational depth.

The wizard, Jared McCarthy of McCarthy Creative, did a magical job of layout and book design. He added creative touches to make it special, because he still knows how to think like a kid!

I want to thank my friend, Joyce Winfield of Writing Resources, who endured many cups of coffee and lemon bars with me as she read and reread with her masterful eyes, proofreading the book.

I wish to thank Tom Goc of Goc Photography, a gifted photographer and college friend, who captured the photo of me used on the book cover.

Many family and friends have offered ongoing support and suggestions: my mom, brother Dale, Aunt Dottie Jacobs, Sarah Keenan, Jim Hiatt, Malissa Bullock, Ginger Rosenthal, Don Bowen, Mike and Tracy Feathers, Maureen Coffey, Scott Wessel, Cody and Katie Ressel, Matt Norman, Stephen Camron, Marty and Sharon Pedersen, Tammy Zinsmeister, Dr. Paul Campbell, Keith and Lisa Terry, Volker Werner of Heinsberg Germany, the students at Highland Elementary in Littleton (Colorado), my friends at the Fremont Tribune, and many others who appreciate the mountain of work it takes to create such a book.

Finally, I wish to thank all the animals that I shared a moment of life with in the wild — wondrous creatures that have no political voices but bring so much beauty to the world. I offer you a prayer of gratitude.

-Dean Jacobs

DEAN JACOBS

Connecting people to cultures, history, and the natural wonders of the world.

Dean Jacobs
Speaker, Author,
Photographer

PO Box 911
Fremont, NE 68026
402.719.7083
dean@deanjacobs.org
www.deanjacobs.org

Introduction

There are about 1.25 million identified species of animals in the world. Scientists estimate another 10-30 million are still waiting to be discovered!

I left pages for you to be one of the scientists who discovers a new animal for the letter "X".

Animals come in all shapes, sizes, and colors. They live in every imaginable habitat all over the world that includes: deserts, rain forests, woodlands, oceans, grasslands, and mountains.

The 25 animals I photographed that are in this book are a small representation of the amazing animals scattered across the world. Perhaps the most important animal is the one that has yet to be discovered by you.

The impact of humans on the changing and destruction of habitat is moving at an ever-quickening pace. If we want to have the privilege to be in awe of all these amazing creatures, we must find a way to protect where they live. This begins with having an appreciation of what animals live where and why.

For each animal, you will learn about its size, habitat, what it eats, and something really cool. You will also learn what its conservation status is and where it can be found in the world. Amy Tharp, an elementary teacher in Colorado, helped craft this information to make it student friendly. The bold words in the text can be found in the glossary.

Finally, you will read in my journal entries what it was like to be with these amazing animals as I took photos of them in the wild.

A world map in the back of the book shows where I was exploring when I photographed these wondrous creatures.

May this book leave you with a sense of awe and a hunger to learn more.

-Dean Jacobs

Table of Contents

"Animals come in all shapes, sizes, and colors.

They live in every imaginable habitat all over the world, including deserts, rain forests, woodlands, oceans, grasslands, and mountains."

A a Albatross
(Galápagos albatross)

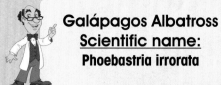

Galápagos Albatross
Scientific name:
Phoebastria irrorata

▲ This is an albatross resting after a long trip. It has the largest wingspan of any bird in the world.

This albatross is flying over the ocean. It likes to eat fresh fish that it catches. Yummy!

Saying "Hello!" with a dance and a kiss. This looks like fun!

Where I Live On Our Planet

Albatross live in the red areas.

Do you notice anything unusual about where they live?

4

Big or small?

If you had to guess which bird has the longest wingspan, what would it be? The eagle? The ostrich? Nope, it's the albatross! With a wingspan of 11 feet, they make a spectacular sight soaring through the sky. Sometimes the albatross will fly for hours without rest or a single flap of its wings. Even with all that wing length, an albatross only weighs around 20 pounds. That's about as much as a small dog or a very large cat!

Habitat:

It's a good thing the albatross have such strong wings because they spend at least 85% of their lives at sea. They are rarely seen on land except during the mating season. This means they spend over 10 months of every year either flying over or floating on the water.

What's for lunch?

Since we know the albatross spend pretty much all of their time near the ocean, it makes sense they mostly eat fish. But did you know they also eat squid? Cool! Albatross are very serious about their food and will even fly more than 10,000 miles to deliver one meal to their chicks.

The wow factor!

Have you ever tried to drink salty water? Yuck! Albatross are one of the only land animals in the world that can drink seawater. This is because they have a very special nose that gets rid of the salt by filtering it out. When the salt drips down the albatross' noses, they look like they are crying or have very bad colds!

How are they doing?

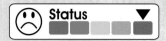

Conservation status:
Critically Endangered

Scientists have officially named 20 species of albatross. Sadly, some albatross species have decreased by 90% since the 1940s; others have decreased by 40-50%. Galápagos albatross are considered critically endangered, mainly because many drown on fishing hooks attached to long fishing lines on the open sea. Their food supply is also threatened by **pollution** such as oil spills.

Dean's Journal...

"For eight days I sailed through the Galápagos Islands, which belong to Ecuador. On one of the Islands, I happened upon a pair of albatross greeting each other with an amazing sort of courting dance.

Watching their heads bob up and down as they slapped their bills back and forth was a sight to behold. It all happened so fast!"

— Dean Jacobs

Bb Blue-Footed Boobie

**Blue-Footed Boobie
Scientific name:**
Sula nebouxii

▲ This is a blue-footed boobie. Did you notice the big, blue feet? That's their natural color! No socks!

The male with the bluest feet is considered the most handsome.

Just resting after a long day of fishing.

"I look a little like a duck. Did you ever see a duck with fancy blue shoes?"

Where I Live On Our Planet

Blue-footed boobies live in the red areas.

Big or small?

Blue-footed boobies weigh just 3.3 pounds yet have a 5-foot wingspan. Can you imagine an animal the size of a guinea pig with wings that are 5-feet wide? Wow!

Habitat:

Blue-footed boobies are found off the western coasts of the Americas, including the Galápagos Islands. They nest on land at night. During the day, they use their amazing wings to soar over the ocean in search of food.

What's for lunch?

You've probably already guessed that blue-footed boobies dine on fish. They mostly feed on school fish like sardines, anchovies, mackerel, and flying fish. Sometimes they even eat squid. What's even more amazing than what they eat is how they catch it. When blue-footed boobies spot a school of fish from up in the air, they fold their long wings back around their bodies. Then they go into a free-fall dive straight down into the water from as high as 80 feet in the air! Look out, fish!

The wow factor!

So what's with the feet? Blue-footed boobies have the most brilliantly colored blue feet of any animal and they aren't even cold! These fabulous feet actually serve a very important purpose . . . to impress the ladies! The males prance around with a high-stepping strut to show off their feet. The male with the bluest feet is considered the most handsome.

How are they doing?

Conservation status:
Least Concern

There are 10 different **species** of the blue-footed boobie. These birds are legally protected on the Galápagos Islands, which is where most of them live. Unfortunately, they are not protected from human disasters, such as oil spills, that pollute their waters. Blue-footed boobies also live on islands in the Pacific Ocean where they are sometimes threatened by people who collect their eggs.

Dean's Journal...

"Walking across one of the Galápagos Islands, I came upon a blue-footed boobie. He was standing in the middle of his nest.

'Interesting place to build a nest,' I thought, 'It's right in the middle of the trail!' He looked up with his silly face and seemed to be asking me to please walk around. So I did!"

— Dean Jacobs

Cc Crocodile
(Nile crocodile)

Nile Crocodile
Scientific name:
Crocodylus niloticus

▲ This is a Nile crocodile. It can be as long as two minivans parked end to end! Wow, that's long!

Nile crocodiles
live in the red areas.

All crocodiles like to swim. They spend most of their time in the water, looking for food.

Here's a family of Nile crocodiles right next to the Nile River. Dean Jacobs' boat was real close to them.

Some crocs are 20-feet long!

8

Big or small?

With an average weight of 500 pounds and somewhere between 100 and 1,000 teeth, Nile crocodiles are easily the scariest creatures in the water. They can even weigh up to 1,650 pounds, which is as heavy as a large cow! Nile crocodiles may not be very tall, but they sure are long. Most are around 16-feet long but some can get up to 20 feet in length. This is about as long as two minivans parked end to end! Yikes!

Habitat:

Similar to American alligators, Nile crocodiles like to hang out in rivers, **freshwater** marshes, and swamps. They are found throughout sub-Saharan Africa, the Nile Basin, and Madagascar.

What's for lunch?

Meeting a 500-pound croc in the wild could be a little scary, and is definitely dangerous, but crocodiles mainly dine on fish. They have been known to hunt together by forming a half-circle across a river to herd the fish. Then they reach out to snatch the fish that are closest to them. Pretty clever! Nile crocodiles can eat up to half their body weight at one time. That's a lot of fish!

The wow factor!

Did you know most reptiles lay their eggs and then take off, never giving their children a second thought? But not the Nile croc! Both the mother and father are caring parents who ferociously guard their nests until the eggs hatch. They will even roll the eggs gently in their mouths to help the hatching baby find its way out.

How are they doing?

Conservation status:
Least Concern

Nile crocodiles are amazingly **resilient.** Even though they were hunted almost to **extinction** about 50 years ago, their numbers are increasing in most areas. This is because laws were passed to protect them from hunters who were after their skins or who were just afraid of them. In some areas, they are still in danger from **pollution**, hunting, and loss of their **habitat**.

Dean's Journal...

"As my boat floated by the banks of the Nile River in Murchison National Park of Uganda, Africa, I noticed they were lined with large crocodiles. I kept thinking to myself, this probably wouldn't be a good place to go for a swim, especially if the crocs were really hungry!"

— Dean Jacobs

Dd Deer
(white-tailed deer)

White-tailed Deer
Scientific name:
Odocoileus virginianus

▲ This is a white-tailed deer. It's very good at hiding in the forest because it has camouflage.

Questions for you.

Can you find where you live on this map?

Are you neighbors with any deer?

Where I Live On Our Planet

White-tailed deer live in the red areas.

Male deer have antlers, or "horns," like the one in the first picture. Female deer do not have antlers.
Which of these deer are male?
Which ones are female?

Big or small?

Are you the smallest person in your family? In your class at school? Well, white-tailed deer are the smallest of the three deer families living in North America. It probably doesn't bother them, though. At around 7-feet long and weighing up to 300 pounds, they are still one of the biggest animals in the woods!

Habitat:

Based on what deer like to eat, it's no surprise they like to hang out in forests. They live in leafy and evergreen forests near meadows where they find grass to add to their diet. Evergreen forests also offer protection from the harsh weather in winter.

What's for lunch?

Have you ever tried to eat part of a tree? You know, chewed on a stick, twirled a leaf on your tongue, or crunched a tree bud? If you have, your stomach probably didn't like it. But not the white-tailed deer! With stomachs of steel, these amazing **herbivores** eat the buds, twigs, leaves, nuts, fruit, and bark of trees. They also eat grass and corn, depending on their **habitat** or the season of the year.

The wow factor!

In the winter, white-tailed deer have faded, grayish-brown fur, but in summer their coats transform to a rich, reddish-brown color. Both colors are helpful in keeping them **camouflaged** from **predators.** Another safety feature of the deer is the white fur on the underside of their tails. When you see the white of their tails sticking straight up like a flag, danger is near!

How are they doing?

Conservation status:
Least Concern

Believe it or not, there are more white-tailed deer in North America today than before European people arrived on the continent. Before that time, deer were hunted by Native Americans, wolves, and mountain lions all year long. Today, deer are hunted by people only during certain times of the year.

Dean's Journal...

"I have canoed the Platte River in Nebraska many times. As I quietly glided down the river near the bank, I often came upon grazing white-tailed deer. Each time the deer gave the same response of being spooked. Then they ran away with their tails standing straight up as if waving good-bye!"

— Dean Jacobs

A
B
C
D
E
F
G
H
I
J
K
L
M
N
O
P
Q
R
S
T
U
V
W
X
Y
Z

Ee Elephant
(African elephant)

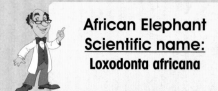

African Elephant
Scientific name:
Loxodonta africana

▲ This is the African elephant. It's huge! Can you imagine an animal the size of a school bus?

Where I Live On Our Planet

African elephants live in the red areas.

Elephants need lots of food. Here's an elephant family that is going out for lunch. One elephant can eat 300 pounds of food in one day!

The white tusks on the elephants are made of ivory. People used to hunt elephants to get their tusks. Now, that's against the law.

12

Big or small?

Standing next to an African elephant is a lot like standing next to a school bus. These **humongous** land animals can grow up to 13-feet tall, 25-feet long, and weigh up to 14,000 pounds. Impressive! How would you like to ride one of these guys to school?

Habitat:

Obviously, African elephants need wide open spaces with a large food supply. They find this on the **savannas** and dry woodlands of Africa. Staying away from humans is a challenge, and it is getting harder as more and more people move into their spaces. Because of this, they often live in wildlife **refuges** where people can go visit them.

What's for lunch?

It's no surprise that African elephants spend a lot of time eating. They even get up in the middle of the night for a snack. You'd eat a lot too if you were a 14,000-pound **vegetarian**! These elephants travel over great distances searching for the roots, grasses, fruit, and bark they need to keep their massive bodies going. An adult elephant can eat around 300 pounds of food in one day. That's a lot of grass!

The wow factor!

Did you know an elephant's trunk has 100,000 different muscles? This is hard to imagine since the human nose doesn't have any muscles at all! This multitude of muscles helps elephants do all sorts of useful things like smelling, breathing, trumpeting, drinking, and grabbing things.

How are they doing?

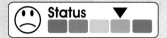

Conservation status: Threatened

At one time, elephants lived throughout Africa. Today they live on less than one-third of the continent. A big reason for their disappearance is people hunt them for their ivory tusks. Luckily, laws have been passed to protect the elephants by making it illegal to sell ivory, although some **poaching** continues. The biggest problem for elephants now is that areas of land with wide-open savannas are being taken over by farmland, ranches, and even deserts.

Dean's Journal...

"As I drove down a dirt path in the Serengeti National Park in Tanzania, a bull elephant approached and pushed the jeep off to the side as if to remind me who was the real boss in Africa."

— Dean Jacobs

F f Flamingo

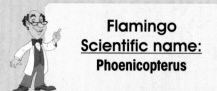

Flamingo
Scientific name:
Phoenicopterus

▲ This bird is a flamingo. Flamingos are about 3- to 4-feet tall. Are you taller or shorter than a flamingo?

Flamingos are found near shallow water. That is where they get their food. When you read the next page, you'll be surprised at how they eat in the water!

Flamingos live in the red areas of Africa.

Flamingos live in some other countries, too!

14

Big or small?

Flamingos are famous for being the only tall, pink birds that live on our planet. Standing 3- to 4-feet tall, they would fit right in with a class of 1st graders. However, they only weigh around 8 pounds, while an average 1st grader weighs about 40 pounds. Big difference!

Habitat:

Flamingos use their long, gangly legs and webbed feet to stir up mud in the bottom of lakes and rivers where they live. They especially like to live in places where rivers meet oceans, and the muddier the water the better. Read the next section to find out why!

What's for lunch?

Mud holds the tasty morsels of food flamingos love. The problem is, how do these clever birds remove their lunch from the gooey black slime? First, they use their long, lean necks to drop their heads just under the surface of muddy water. Then, they turn their heads slightly sideways and suck up a big hunk of mud in their bent bills. Next, they pump out the mud and eat the food that's left behind. The food can be any tasty assortment of **algae, larvae,** adult insects, small fish, or **crustaceans.** Eeeeww!

The wow factor!

You may be wondering how flamingos get all that mud out of their bills. These birds can pump water through their bills 20 times a second! Think about that for a second. See, a second isn't very long, is it? All this pumping happens so fast that scientists didn't even know flamingos could do it until slow-motion photography was invented.

How are they doing?

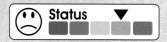

Conservation status: Threatened

Five million flamingos live in the world today. That sounds like a lot, doesn't it? Think about this, though. There are only around 30 breeding and nesting sites on our planet for all these birds. That's not very many! Also, the **habitat** of these birds is threatened when people build dams or drain lakes. This changes the depth of the water, which makes it hard for flamingos to eat. For example, when a river or lake gets too deep, flamingos can't eat because they need shallow, muddy water.

Dean's Journal...

"As my jeep came over a ridge in Kenya, Africa, I looked at the lake below. The sight took my breath away because covering almost half of the lake was a vibrant pink, as thousands of feeding flamingos waded through the shallow water."

— Dean Jacobs

Gg Gorilla
(mountain gorilla)

Gorilla
Scientific name:
Gorilla beringei beringei

▲ This is a family of mountain gorillas. The little baby gorilla may grow to weigh 450 pounds!

Wow! Here's Dean Jacobs taking pictures of the gorillas in Rwanda, Africa.

The little gorilla is just a baby. He loves to get rides from his mother and father.

This is an adult gorilla. He can eat 50 pounds of plants in one day!

Where I Live On Our Planet

Mountain gorillas live in the red areas of Uganda, Rwanda, and The Democratic Republic of the Congo.

Big or small?

Mountain gorillas can grow up to 6-feet tall, which is about the same height as a man. An average man, however, weighs about 190 pounds while a male mountain gorilla can weigh up to 450 pounds. As you can guess, all this added weight makes mountain gorillas very strong!

Habitat:

Have you ever thought about living on a volcano in the middle of a rain forest? This is exactly where the mountain gorillas live! Luckily for them, these volcanoes, called the Virungas, are **dormant**, which means they don't erupt anymore. The plants gorillas love to eat grow in large numbers on the sides of these volcanic mountains in central Africa.

What's for lunch?

Mountain gorillas are very clever plant eaters, or **herbivores**. Not only do they eat 200 different types of plants, but they also eat many plant parts. These parts include the leaves, shoots, stems, fruit, flowers, and even bark. What's more, they eat 45-50 pounds of this plant material each day! Because these plants have lots of water in them, mountain gorillas hardly ever need to drink water.

The wow factor!

Because mountain gorillas live in a cold and misty **environment**, their fur is long and thick. Male gorillas over the age of 11 grow a large patch of silver hair on their backs. At this point, they are called silverbacks. Gorillas take care of their useful coats by grooming each other.

How are they doing?

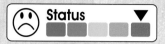

Conservation status:
Critically Endangered

Only about 782 mountain gorillas live on our planet today. Do you know how many people live on our planet? About 6.6 billion! Hmmm ... big difference! There aren't many mountain gorillas because much of their **habitat** has been turned into farmland to feed all those people. They have also been hunted **illegally** for their body parts over the past several decades. Luckily, the mountain gorillas now have three **national parks** to live in and are watched over carefully by scientists. In recent years, their numbers have actually grown.

Dean's Journal...

"One morning my friends and I spent three hours climbing the side of a volcano in Rwanda, Africa to find mountain gorillas. When we finally found them, we made a gorilla sound to let them know we were their friends. They looked up at us curiously, then went back to their task of eating plants as if we weren't even there."

— Dean Jacobs

A B C D E F G **H** I J K L M N O P Q R S T U V W X Y Z

Hh Hippopotamus

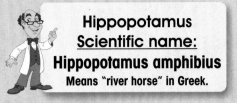

**Hippopotamus
Scientific name:
Hippopotamus amphibius**
Means "river horse" in Greek.

▲ This is a hippopotamus. Its name comes from the Greek term for "river horse," but don't try to ride one!

Where I Live On Our Planet

Hippos live in the tiny red areas of Africa.

Hippos used to live in the light green area, too.

Hippos live near the water of rivers and lakes. The water helps them keep cool. Can you imagine finding a hippo keeping cool in a swimming pool? Yikes!

This is a hippo family. They are probably getting out of the river so they can get some lunch. Read the next page to find out what they eat.

Big or small?

Hippos are big, hefty animals. They can weigh at least 5,000 pounds and measure up to 15-feet long, which is about the same size as a car. Hmm... what would it be like to have one of these big guys parked in the garage?

Habitat:

Hippos don't care for garages, though. They much prefer the deep water of rivers and lakes. Throw in a bunch of reed beds with a grassland nearby and you have many happy hippos!

What's for lunch?

Cars need gas; hippos need grass. And lots of it! If you've ever pulled up a handful of grass on a warm summer day and let it slip through your fingers, then you know how light it is. Hippos can eat 100 pounds of grass every day!

The wow factor!

Can hippos sweat blood? Some people used to think so. When hippos come out of deep water to be in the sun on the edge of a river or lake, their skin gives off an oily red liquid. It has nothing to do with blood, though. It's really the hippos' own natural sun block and skin lotion. Cool!

How are they doing?

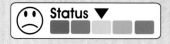

Conservation status: Vulnerable

The number of hippos in our world is declining. Reasons for this are hunting and losing their **habitat**. People hunt hippos for their ivory tusks, for their meat, or because people are afraid of how **ferocious** hippos are. They are often considered the most aggressive animal in Africa. In some areas, they are hunted simply to reduce the **population** because there are too many hippos and not enough food for all of them.

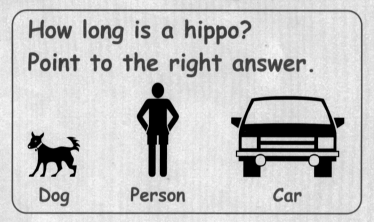

How long is a hippo?
Point to the right answer.

Dog   Person   Car

Dean's Journal...

"Hippos were lined along the bank of the Nile River in Uganda, Africa like parked cars in downtown main street America. They occasionally opened their large mouths to yawn as I floated by in my large boat."

— Dean Jacobs

Ii Iguana

Iguana
Scientific name:
Amblyrhynchus cristatus
(marine iguana)

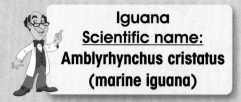

▲ This is a Galápagos land iguana. Read the next page to learn about Galápagos marine iguanas!

Marine iguanas only live on the Galápagos Islands. These iguanas are getting a little sun!

These marine iguanas found a friend. Is the friend a dog? A bird? A crab? If you said "crab," you're right!

Where I Live On Our Planet

Marine iguanas live in the tiny red area inside the circle.

A B C D E F G H I J K L M N O P Q R S T U V W X Y Z

Big or small?

Marine iguanas are long, skinny, and ugly. One of the first people ever to write about them even called them "hideous-looking." Well, look at the pictures and decide for yourself. An amazing thing about the size of marine iguanas is they can grow up to 5-feet long, but their weight is only around 3 pounds. Can you picture how skinny a 5-foot-tall person would be if he or she only weighed 3 pounds!!!?

Habitat:

Marine iguanas are found only on the volcanic islands of the Galápagos. These Islands make a great **habitat** because they have the steep rock cliffs and sandy beaches these iguanas need for nesting.

What's for lunch?

Maybe the reason marine iguanas are so skinny is because they are **vegetarians** that mostly eat seaweed and **algae**. They work hard to get at the algae because it sticks to rocks like glue. Luckily, these iguanas have small, razor-sharp teeth that help with the tricky task of scraping it off.

The wow factor!

An amazing thing about marine iguanas is the way their bodies handle salt. Think about it – the seaweed they eat grows in salt water. So every time they take a bite, in comes a mouthful of salt. To get rid of all this salt, iguanas have a gland between their eyes and nose that filters it out. One more thing has to happen before the salt is finally removed from the body. Iguanas have to sneeze! This causes the salt to land on the iguanas' heads, making them look like they're wearing white wigs.

How are they doing?

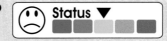

Conservation status: Vulnerable

Laws throughout the Galápagos Islands protect marine iguanas, but they are still in some danger of becoming **extinct**. Water **pollution** due to oil spills is a problem for them. In addition, the dogs, cats, and rats that also live on the islands often **prey** on iguana eggs and the young.

Dean's Journal...

"Often as I was exploring the Galápagos Islands, I would see marine iguanas spread across the rocks. With grins on their faces, they sunned themselves in the afternoon light. Just to remind me they were alive, salt would suddenly come blowing out their noses before they dozed back to sleep."

— Dean Jacobs

Jj Jackal
(black-backed jackal)

Jackal
Scientific name:
Canis mesomelas

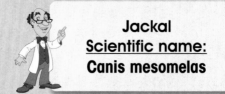

▲ This is a black-backed jackal. The jackal's coloring and camouflage helps protect it from predators.

Here we find Dean Jacobs on an African mountaintop along the Nile River. He is looking for more places to find animals so he can share the photos with you!

It looks like there are two black-backed jackals, but the one that looks upside-down is really a reflection in the water. This jackal was out for a night-time walk.

Where I Live On Our Planet

Jackals live in the red areas of Africa and the Middle East.

22

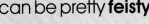

Big or small?
Black-backed jackals look like lean, wiry, 1½-foot-tall dogs. With their pointed noses and long pointed ears, they look cute enough to take home. Don't try to keep one for a pet, though. Despite their small size, all 22 pounds of them can be pretty **feisty**!

Habitat:
Even though they wouldn't make such great pets, black-backed jackals often live close to people. They can be found in smaller cities or the **suburbs** of large cities. Mostly, though, they prefer the open **savannas** and woodlands of central and southern Africa.

What's for lunch?
Black-backed jackals are **omnivores** that enjoy a wide variety of food. This can range from small antelope, **reptiles**, and **rodents** to fruit, grass, and insects. Because jackals sometimes live near people, they have been known to visit the local dump for a quick take-out meal.

The wow factor!
If you've ever spent time on a school playground, you know what it's like to hang out with a pack of black-backed jackals. Jackals are noisy! They communicate with each other through screaming yells, lots of yapping, and a siren-like howl when food is located. Hmmm . . . sound familiar?

How are they doing?

Conservation status:
Stable
Black-backed jackals are not in danger of **extinction** because they can adapt so easily to many different **environments**. The main problem for jackals is that humans are moving into their **habitats** and taking over. At some point, there may not be room for everyone!

How big is a jackal?
Point to the right answer.

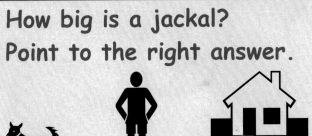

Dog   Person   House

Dean's Journal...

"On a trek through Namibia, Africa, I was lucky enough to spot a black-backed jackal. My truck slowly came to a stop as I watched the jackal work its way across the shallow waters looking for food. The still waters offered a beautiful reflection of the graceful jackal."

— Dean Jacobs

Kk Koala

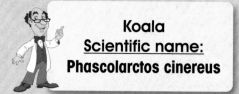

Koala
Scientific name:
Phascolarctos cinereus

▲ This koala is way up in a eucalyptus tree, eating the only food that it likes – eucalyptus leaves!

Where I Live On Our Planet

Koalas live in the red area of Eastern Australia.

Australia

This is the Australian outback where Dean Jacobs found koalas. Notice how high the mountains are. That took a lot of climbing!

Be careful! Don't ever eat eucalyptus leaves. They are poisonous, but the koalas can eat them and not get sick. Find out why on the next page.

Can you figure out why Australia is called the Land Down Under? See the big map in the back of the book to see where Australia is to find out!

Big or small?

Koalas are **marsupials** that start their lives the size of a jellybean snuggled up in their mothers' pouches. When they are all grown up, they weigh around 25 pounds and are about 2½-feet tall. Cute, round teddy bears is what they remind us of. Don't try to cuddle up with one, though. Koalas can be pretty **feisty** and they like to live alone.

Habitat:

Koalas can only be found in the eucalyptus forests of eastern Australia. They spend most of their days up in the trees sleeping, resting, and eating. They move very slowly and seem to have a lazy lifestyle. They aren't really lazy, though. It just takes a lot of energy for their bodies to **digest** all those tough eucalyptus leaves!

What's for lunch?

Koalas are very picky eaters. They only eat eucalyptus leaves! Zookeepers have tried to give them other kinds of food, like carrots, but they won't touch any of it. It's amazing that koalas can even eat eucalyptus since the leaves are poisonous to most other animals. They can eat these **toxic** leaves because their stomachs have **adapted** over time to remove the poisons.

The wow factor!

From the time they are born, koalas are excellent climbers. At first, baby koalas climb around inside their mothers' pouches. When they get old enough to leave the pouches, they climb onto their mothers' backs. Then the baby koalas hold on with strong hands and feet. After a year, the koala babies are ready to climb eucalyptus trees and live on their own. To help with all this climbing, koalas have two thumbs on each hand, ridges on the bottoms of their feet, and claws on both hands and feet.

How are they doing?

Conservation status:

Least Concern

The biggest threat to koalas is loss of their **habitat** to houses, farms, malls, parking lots, and other human needs. Roads are also a big problem. They cut through the forests, making it hard for males and females to find each other during mating season. Many koalas get run over because they move so slowly across the road. But people are helping. They are creating special places for koalas to live that are protected from roads and other human activity. Currently, koalas are holding their own in the Land Down Under.

Dean's Journal...

"While driving my car on the back roads of Australia, I pulled off to the side so I could step out and stretch for a moment. As I was stretching my arms, I glanced up and saw a koala taking a nap in a tree. I thought to myself, 'I wish I could take a nap in a tree, too.' Wouldn't that be fun!"

— Dean Jacobs

L l Leopard
(African leopard)

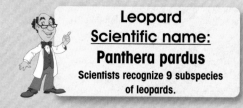
Leopard
Scientific name:
Panthera pardus
Scientists recognize 9 subspecies
of leopards.

▲ This is a leopard that was taking his catnap on some big rocks in Tanzania, Africa.

Where I Live On Our Planet
Leopards live in the red areas of the map.

Leopards have very fancy fur! The spots help them to hide from predators and to sneak up on their lunch.

Most cats don't like to swim. Leopards are part of the cat family, but they love to swim and play in the water. Do you think their spots come off when they take a bath?

Big or small?
Leopards are unique in the world of cats. Not only can they climb trees, but they can climb 50 feet up a tree carrying a dead animal that weighs more than they do! Since their average weight is 130 pounds, you can imagine how big an animal that might be! Also, leopards are around 5-feet long but can leap forward 20 feet in a single bound. How many feet forward can you jump?

Habitat:
Obviously, most leopards like to live in areas where there are trees. But leopards are highly **adaptable** to many different **environments,** both warm and cold. They feel just as comfortable in swampy tropical forests as in rugged mountains. They can also be found in lowland forests, grasslands, brush country, and deserts.

What's for lunch?
Are you wondering what kinds of animals leopards carry up a tree? Leopards are **carnivores** that eat a wide variety of meat, depending on what is available in their area. They have been known to hunt anything from fish, **reptiles**, and birds to **mammals** such as **rodents**, hares, warthogs, antelope, monkeys, and baboons.

The wow factor!
Cats in general are well known for their dislike of water. But not the leopard! Leopards actually enjoy water and are very strong swimmers.

How are they doing?
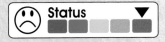

Conservation status:
Threatened to Critically Endangered
The fact that leopards are highly adaptable to different environments has certainly helped them survive. They still face many problems, however. Like most wild animals, their **habitat** is being destroyed by humans moving in. They have also been hunted almost to **extinction** in some areas for their fur or as trophies.

Dean's Journal...
"After hours of driving across the open Serengeti in Africa, I came to a large group of boulders that were surrounded by trees in the middle of nowhere. It looked just like the rock outcrop from the movie, 'The Lion King.' Resting on top of one of the boulders was a leopard. The leopard casually blinked a few times at my presence before quickly slumbering back to his catnap."

— Dean Jacobs

Mm Monkey
(golden monkey)

Monkey
Scientific name:
Cercopithecus kandti
Scientists recognize approximately 130 species of monkeys.

▲ Wow! One of the rarest kinds of monkeys in the world is looking right into the camera. He's a real show-off.

Where I Live On Our Planet
Golden monkeys live in the red area of Africa.

It looks like Dean Jacobs has made some new friends. These little monkeys climbed on him like he was a tree!

Little golden monkeys are neighbors with the great big mountain gorillas.
They all live in Rwanda, Africa.

Golden monkeys like to eat plants. Sometimes they even eat bugs!

28

Big or small?

Many different types of monkeys live in the world today – over 130 different types, in fact! These monkeys can weigh as little as 4 ounces (a quarter of a pound) or as much as 77 pounds. Golden monkeys show up on the smaller end of the scale at 10-25 pounds. They happen to be one of the rarest monkeys in the world.

Habitat:

Golden monkeys can only be found in one place in the world, which is why they are so rare. In order to see a golden monkey in the wild, you would travel to the volcanic mountains of the Virunga National Park in Rwanda, Africa. Here you would find them running along the tops of the trees in the thick bamboo forests that grow on the sides of the volcanoes. Do you remember which other well-known animal lives here? Right, mountain gorillas!

What's for lunch?

Like the mountain gorillas that share their **habitat,** golden monkeys eat many different kinds of leaves and other parts of the plants that grow in their **environment.** They especially like fruit and will even eat insects from time to time.

The wow factor!

A big difference between golden monkeys and their mountain gorilla neighbors is that monkeys have tails and the gorillas, which are part of the ape family, do not. Golden monkeys use their tails for balance and for swinging through the trees.

How are they doing?

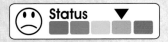

Conservation status:
Endangered

Because golden monkeys and mountain gorillas share the same limited habitat, they share the same dangers. A big threat is loss of their habitat due to people using the land for farms. Poachers also set traps for antelope in the park where they live. Monkeys can get caught in these traps, too.

Dean's Journal...

"Weaving my way through the thick bamboo forest was exciting. I couldn't see very far, but an occasional screech told me I was on the right path to find the rare golden monkeys. Suddenly, jumping from the tops of the bamboo, there was a troop of monkeys welcoming me to the Volcanoes National Park in Rwanda, Africa."

— Dean Jacobs

Nn Newt
(fire bellied newt)

Fire Bellied Newt
Scientific name:
Cynops orientalis
There are hundreds of different species of newts found all over the world.

▲ This fire bellied newt is really only 4-inches long. He likes to swim and eat in cold water lakes.

This shows you how tiny the newt is. It is soft and slippery to hold!

This is an adult newt with its baby. Can you see that the baby's skin is much smoother than the bumpy skin of the adult?

Newts have eyes on the sides of their heads so they can see more around them. Just like frogs!

Where I Live On Our Planet

Fire bellied newts are found in the red area of China.

Big or small?

Fire bellied newts begin their lives as **larvae**, in other words white gooey worms. These little guys live in water. They swim around all day eating **algae** and tiny bugs. Eventually all this eating transforms them, two legs at a time, into full-grown, 4-inch long, fire bellied newts. Big change, huh?

Habitat:

Fire bellied newts are just one of hundreds of different kinds of newts found around the world. This particular type of newt is native to China. They need **freshwater** to live in. The water can be just about anywhere such as ponds, brooks, flooded fields, wells, and ditches. The best kind of water for newts is cold and quiet, in the shade, and has a mud bottom.

What's for lunch?

Fire bellied newts actively hunt for, and even **ambush**, their **prey.** Although scientists don't know everything about what fire bellied newts eat, they can guess that these newts would enjoy things like worms, **larvae**, and eggs.

The wow factor!

Because fire bellied newts have soft bodies, they may seem **vulnerable** to **predators**. Luckily for them, however, they have a very effective form of defense . . . poison! The reason their poison works so well is that it oozes right out of their skin like toothpaste out of a tube. Even though predators can't see the poison, the bright red or yellow markings on the stomach of the newt sends a great big warning to stay away.

How are they doing?

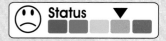

Conservation status:

Threatened

As with many animal **species** across the globe, newts are threatened by human activity. For example, the natural forests where newts live are often replaced by farms. Instead of living in natural ponds, many newts are now forced to live in water that has drained from the fields. This water is often polluted with the chemicals used for farming.

Dean's Journal...

"Fire bellied newts come from China. When I was in China it was winter; this means frozen water. Not the best time to go newt hunting! I've never seen a newt in the wild. These photos were taken from the wilds of my home in Nebraska! I ordered them from the pet store."

— Dean Jacobs

Oo Orangutan
(Sumatran orangutan)

Sumatran Orangutan
Scientific name:
Pongo abelii
There are 2 subspecies
of orangutans in the world.

▲ Here's an adult and a baby orangutan. It looks like they might be enjoying a banana for lunch.

Where I Live On Our Planet

Orangutans live in the red areas of Indonesia.

This orangutan is fully grown. It can weigh as much as 250 pounds!

This is an orangutan with a baby. It looks like the baby is picking out its lunch from a tree!

Orangutans love to spend time in trees. Just look at how long their arms are. Their long arms help them climb.

Big or small?

Full-grown orangutans are just slightly smaller than an adult human. Their average height is between 4- and 5-feet tall and their average weight is 127 pounds. Some male orangutans can weigh as much as 250 pounds. Take a look at orangutans' arms. Pretty long, aren't they? They are actually twice as long as their legs and can measure 7 feet from fingertip to fingertip.

Habitat:

Orangutans would be very comfortable in a tree house since they live almost completely in trees. They even build their nests in trees like a bird! They used to live in rain forests throughout Indonesia, but today they are found on only two of the islands.

What's for lunch?

Which do you like better, fruit or dirt? Can you believe orangutans eat both! Fruit makes up most of their diet but they also eat leaves, insects, honey, bird eggs, bark, and yes, even dirt! For orangutans, eating dirt is like eating a giant vitamin. The soil adds important minerals to their diet and can even make them feel better when they are sick.

The wow factor!

A human-like **characteristic** of these unique animals is their **opposable** thumb. Orangutans can move their thumbs around like we can, which makes it a snap to pick things up. You can check that out by taping your thumb to your hand and trying to pick up a pencil. Then try it using your thumb, too. Which way do you think is easier?

How are they doing?

Conservation status:
Critically Endangered

Orangutans have lost 80% of their **habitat** in the past 20 years. This would be like an elementary school losing every 2nd, 3rd, 4th, and 5th grade classroom. Can you imagine all those students now having class in just the kindergarten and 1st grade classrooms? Yikes!

Orangutans are losing their habitat from loggers cutting down the forests they live in. Loggers turn this land into farms where the orangutans can't live. They are also losing their habitat to forest fires and roads that cut through their land.

Dean's Journal...

"For an hour I hiked through the jungle looking for orangutans. Eventually, I spotted them high in the treetops. The orangutans swung through the trees in the Sumatran jungle of Indonesia with a quietness, gracefulness, and beauty that reminded me of ballet dancers."

— Dean Jacobs

P p Panda
(giant panda)

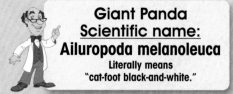

Giant Panda
Scientific name:
Ailuropoda melanoleuca
Literally means
"cat-foot black-and-white."

▲ This is a giant panda. Can you guess what it likes to eat? Bamboo! The next page tells you how much.

Giant pandas live in the red areas of China.

A giant panda is only as big as a stick of butter when it is born.

Here is a family of giant pandas. They have special thumbs that help them eat. The next page tells you why!

This giant panda is having lunch and playing at the same time. What fun!

A B C D E F G H I J K L M N O P Q R S T U V W X Y Z

34

Big or small?

Giant pandas don't start out as giants. When they are born, these pandas are only as big as a stick of butter! They grow fast, though, and in about two years, pandas can weigh from 220 to 330 pounds and be 4- to 5-feet long. That's a pretty big stick of butter!

Habitat:

You can probably guess where giant pandas like to live. Yep, bamboo forests! These forests are located in mountain areas in the middle of China. These forests can be as high as 13,000 feet. They are cool and wet – perfect for pandas with their thick, wooly coats.

What's for lunch?

All this weight gain comes from eating lots of bamboo. In fact, giant pandas spend over half their days eating bamboo. This is a little strange because giant pandas actually have the stomach of a **carnivore.** Sometimes they do eat birds or **rodents**, but mostly it's just bamboo.

The wow factor!

Special body parts help giant pandas eat the bamboo they crave. In addition to five fingers, they have a special thumb that allows them to hold the long, slender stalks. Large molar teeth and strong jaws help cut through the tough, chewy stems.

How are they doing?

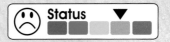

Conservation status: Endangered

Giant pandas used to live in lowland areas of China, as well as remote mountain areas. Most of their lowland **habitat** has now been destroyed by farmers or others who need the land. It is important to save as much of the pandas' natural habitat as possible so their **species** can survive.

Dean's Journal...

"It is impossible not to fall in love with baby pandas. I smiled with delight as I watched them play, tumble, and bend their bodies like a Gumby doll at the Chengdu Panda Reserve.

Being in China during the cold winter gave me a new appreciation of why the pandas have such thick fur."

— Dean Jacobs

Q q Quail
(bobwhite quail)

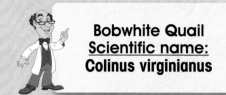

Bobwhite Quail
Scientific name:
Colinus virginianus

▲ This is a bobwhite quail. It is very good at hiding, so you have to watch closely to find a quail!

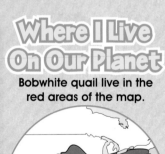

Where I Live On Our Planet

Bobwhite quail live in the red areas of the map.

This is an adult quail and it only weighs about half a pound. It can fly very fast but not very far. It makes a noise like a soft clapping when it flies.

If you are near a river or stream, keep your eyes open to spot bobwhite quail. They like to stay in the low areas and in bushes and tall grass for protection. Can you find the quail standing next to the water?

They also live in Africa, Asia, and Australia!

36

Big or small?

Bobwhite quail are small birds. When first hatched, they weigh less than half an ounce. Even though they grow very quickly, their adult weight is still less than half a pound, which is about as heavy as an orange. Their wingspan of about 4 inches allows them to fly but only for short distances.

Habitat:

Bobwhite quail prefer to live along rivers and streams because these are lowland areas with protection from the wind. Living near water also provides bushy plants for the quail to live in. These plants offer a place for quail to hide from **predators.** Some bobwhite quail also live close to farms because the fences provide the same type of protection as river bottoms.

What's for lunch?

Bobwhite quail are birds that live on the ground. This is also where they find their food. In the spring, quail like to eat new plants that are starting to grow. In the summer, they add insects to their meals. They eat seeds from different kinds of weeds all year long, such as ragweed and beggarweed.

The wow factor!

Since bobwhite quail live on the ground, they are very easy **prey** for **carnivores** such as foxes, coyotes,

and hawks. In fact, 80% of **hatchlings** don't survive. A clever thing the parents do to protect their young when a predator is coming is to pretend to have a broken wing. The predator will then follow the bird that is pretending to be hurt while the babies run the other way!

How are they doing?

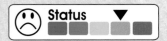

Conservation status:

Endangered

The number of bobwhite quail is **declining** mainly because small farms are turning into bigger farms with fewer fences. This takes away the **habitat** quail need to survive. Bobwhite hatchlings also have a hard time surviving because they get cold easily, often catch diseases, and are hunted by many predators in the wild.

Dean's Journal...

"One of the most beautiful sounds I enjoy when going for a walk in the countryside of Nebraska is the call of the bobwhite quail looking for its mate."

— Dean Jacobs

R r Rabbit

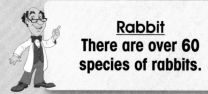

▲ This is an angora rabbit. Just imagine how soft the fur is. The angora rabbit's fur can be made into wool.

Where I Live On Our Planet

Rabbits live in every part of the world.

Rabbits, like this cottontail, love to eat grass, leaves, and sometimes even the fruits and vegetables in your garden. Better put up a fence before lunch!

This is a cottontail rabbit that you might find near your home. But did you know there are over 60 species of rabbits found all over the world? Wow, that sure is a lot of bunnies!

Big or small?

Rabbits come in many different shapes, sizes, and colors. Some are wild and some are tame. Angora rabbits are tame rabbits that can weigh anywhere from 4 to 12 pounds. What makes angora rabbits different from other rabbits is their fur. The long, plush texture makes them not only look adorable, but their fur can also be spun into a special kind of wool. If you've ever had an angora sweater, you know just how special it is!

Habitat:

Rabbits can be found in parts of the world with meadows, woods, forests, thickets, grasslands, deserts, and wetlands. Basically, rabbits can live almost anywhere! Angora rabbits are **domesticated**, which means they can live with people just like a dog or a cat. These rabbits make wonderful pets since they are active, playful, have lots of personality, and like to be with people. People also raise them like sheep . . . for their wool!

What's for lunch?

Rabbits in the wild are **herbivores** with a diverse diet of grasses, leaves, buds, tree bark, and roots. Angora rabbits are fed high fiber pellets, hay, and straw. These foods help angora rabbits **digest** the fur they swallow when they clean themselves. Pineapple juice also helps dissolve the balls of wool that can build up in their stomachs.

The wow factor!

Like all rabbits, angora rabbits are very social. They like to hang out with other rabbits, animals, and people. They especially enjoy playing with toys. So if you ever get an angora for a pet, keep lots of balls and playthings around!

How are they doing?

Conservation status:

Some Threatened / Others Low Concern

Rabbits are members of the **rodent** family, which means there are a lot of them! Would you believe there are more than 60 different **species** of rabbits around the world? Because they are so numerous, rabbits are not highly threatened, except in areas where their **habitat** is being taken over by humans.

Dean's Journal...

"I have friends who have rabbits as pets. Some rabbits even live in the house with their owners. For sure, rabbits have a capacity to bring a smile to your face, especially when they are baby bunnies."

— Dean Jacobs

Ss Sea Lion
(Galápagos sea lion)

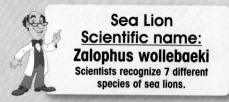

Sea Lion
Scientific name:
Zalophus wollebaeki
Scientists recognize 7 different species of sea lions.

▲ This is a Galápagos sea lion. See the little tiny ear? This is one way to know if you are looking at a sea lion or a seal. Seals' ears don't stick out. Sea lions' ears do. Long whiskers help it navigate in dark water.

Where I Live On Our Planet
You will find these sea lions on the Galápagos Islands.

It looks like nap time. Since sea lions spend so much time swimming, they need a lot of rest. Just like you!

If you were on the beach with these sea lions, you would hear them talking to each other. Read the next page to find out the interesting way that they communicate!

40

Big or small?

In the animal world, it is not unusual for males to be larger than females. What is unusual about sea lions, though, is how much bigger the males are. Male sea lions can weigh up to 2,200 pounds, while female sea lions only weigh up to 600 pounds. Male sea lions use their large size to protect their families from harm.

Habitat:

Sea lions can be found on the rocky, rugged shorelines and gentle, sandy ocean beaches throughout the world. Most live in extremely cold, Arctic areas, but some do prefer warm, tropical waters. You won't find any in the Atlantic Ocean, though, and scientists have no idea why. Maybe some day you can become a scientist and discover the answer to this mystery!

What's for lunch?

Because sea lions live near the ocean, they eat plenty of fish and other types of sea life such as squid, crabs, and clams. Galápagos sea lions also feed on sardines. In fact, they like sardines so much that they will swim over 10 miles out into the ocean to find them. Sea lions eat their seafood by tossing it up in the air. They catch it in the back of their mouths, crush it with their teeth, and swallow it nearly whole. Does that sound like a fun way to eat?

The wow factor!

Sea lions are not shy! They will tell you exactly what they are thinking with all kinds of barks, honks, trumpets, and roars. It is hard to imagine how sea lions make any sense out of all this noise. But they do! In fact, baby sea lions can recognize their mothers' voices from among hundreds of sea lions.

How are they doing?

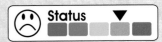

Conservation status:
Endangered

For many years, sea lions were hunted for their skin and oil. Fishermen also shot sea lions because they were damaging their nets. Because of all this hunting, sea lions were wiped out in some areas. **Pollution** from trash and oil spills is also a problem for the Galápagos sea lions. International protection laws have helped, and in some parts of the world sea lions are actually growing in numbers.

Dean's Journal...

"One morning I went snorkeling in the Galápagos Islands. As I swam next to a rock outcrop, suddenly a sea lion pup came swimming right up to my snorkel mask, growled, and dove underneath me in a blink of an eye."

— Dean Jacobs

Tt Tasmanian Devil

Tasmanian Devil
Scientific name:
Sarcophilus harrisii

▲ This is a Tasmanian devil. Wow, look at those teeth. Stay back, they are always hungry!

Where I Live On Our Planet

Tasmanian devils live on the Australian island of Tasmania.

Australia

This Tasmanian devil can grow to 26 pounds. But can you guess how small it was when it was born? Here's a hint: You might enjoy them on your oatmeal. Read the next page to find the answer!

Tasmanian devils are ferocious hunters and eaters. If you see one, don't try to pet it!

Big or small?

Like the koala, Tasmanian devils are members of the amazing **marsupial** family. Their babies start out small and helpless, even the size of a raisin, yet quickly grow into a much larger animal. Tasmanian devils, for example, can grow to be 30-inches long and weigh up to 26 pounds. That's a lot bigger than a raisin!

Habitat:

It's easy to remember where Tasmanian devils live. In Tasmania, of course! Tasmania is an island right below the mainland of Australia. The devils live all over the island but prefer coastal **scrublands** and forests.

What's for lunch?

Tasmanian devils can actually grow to be many different sizes, depending on how much food is in their **environment**. They are not picky eaters. As **carnivores** they hunt **prey** such as snakes, birds, fish, **rodents**, and insects. But if none of these treats are around, they will eat just about any kind of meat, no matter how old or rotten!

The wow factor!

Do you always eat every single bite of food on your plate? Tasmanian devils do! They eat every single part of the animal they are feasting on: bones, guts, fur, teeth, and all! As you can see, devils are serious about their feasting. Maybe that's because they have the strongest bite of any **mammal** in the world. They will often gather in large groups to devour a whole **carcass**. They aren't quiet about it either. They use 11 different sounds to growl, snarl, and yip at each other while eating.

How are they doing?

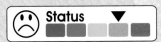

Conservation status:
Endangered

Did you know that Tasmanian devils once lived throughout Australia as well as Tasmania? Farmers in Australia used to kill Tasmanian devils to keep them from hunting their livestock. Eventually, the devil **population** became so small that the government passed laws to protect them. The biggest threat to devils now is a disease that causes tumors on their faces. This **cancer** quickly spreads from one devil to another when they bite each other.

Dean's Journal...

"Listening to the temperamental Tasmanian devils growl and fight over a dead carcass made it clear why they are known as the vacuum cleaners of Tasmania."

— Dean Jacobs

U u Urchin
(sea urchin)

Sea Urchin
Scientific name:
Strongylocentrotus

▲ This is a sea urchin. Sea urchins are very colorful and live in every ocean of the world.

This is Dean Jacobs looking for sea urchins in a Pacific Ocean tidal pool in Oregon.

Urchins live on coral and at the bottom of the ocean. They blend into the scenery quite well!

Urchins are pretty to look at, but they have sharp spines to protect themselves. Ouch!

Where I Live On Our Planet

Urchins live in the oceans in every part of the world.

Big or small?

When looking at sea urchins, the first thing you'll notice is their tall, sharp spikes. This is because the spikes can be as long as the urchin is wide. Yikes! Luckily, sea urchins usually only grow to be 1 to 4 inches in length. Be careful if you go to the Caribbean, though, because sea urchins in this part of the world can have spikes as long as 14 inches!

Habitat:

Sea urchins live in all oceans of the world. They mostly live on coral, but they can also be found on the ocean floor near **kelp** forests. They are tough little creatures that can survive strong waves and churning water.

What's for lunch?

Sea urchins' mouths are on the underside of their bodies. They like to feed on **algae**, but they will also eat other sea creatures such as starfish, clams, and sponges. Sea urchins spend their days moving slowly across coral reefs on hundreds of sticky, tube-like feet, eating all the algae they can find along the way.

The wow factor!

The bodies of sea urchins may not taste very good, but their eggs sure do! People use the urchins' eggs to make a food called caviar, which some think is extra yummy. How would you like to find some urchin eggs in your lunchbox tomorrow?

How are they doing?

Conservation status:
Least Concern

Certain parts of the ocean actually have too many sea urchins. Urchins can **devastate** an **ecosystem** because they strip coral of the precious algae other animals need to survive. In some areas, people have created a solution by adding urchin-eating lobsters and sea otters to the waters.

Dean's Journal...

"People eat urchins. Although looking at them with all those pointy spines, I can't help but wonder why. I calculated the best time to look for sea urchins along the Oregon coastline of the Pacific Ocean by determining when the low tide would happen. As the ocean receded, it left small tidal pools teeming with all kinds of wonderful creatures to explore. But just to remind me the ocean was boss, as I waded in a tidal pool a wave rolled in and went over the top of my rubber boots filling them with seawater."

— Dean Jacobs

Vv Vulture
(Old World vulture)

Vulture
Vultures are classified as either Old World or New World vultures.

▲ These are Old World vultures. They are very big birds that look a bit like turkeys. Look at their long necks!

These vultures are looking for food. Sometimes scientists call that "foraging."

These vultures are doing what they do best. They are removing a dead animal by eating it. This helps keep the environment clean. "Thank you for doing such a nasty job!"

It looks like this vulture likes posing for the camera. His wings can be as wide as 10 feet from tip to tip!

Where I Live On Our Planet

Old World vultures live in the red areas.

Big or small?

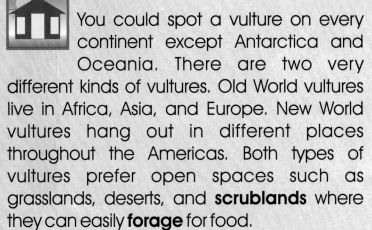

As with many other animal **species**, vultures come in different sizes. They can weigh anywhere from 4 to 31 pounds and have a 5- to 10-foot wingspan. Something that is different about vultures from most other birds is they have no feathers on their heads and necks.

Habitat:

You could spot a vulture on every continent except Antarctica and Oceania. There are two very different kinds of vultures. Old World vultures live in Africa, Asia, and Europe. New World vultures hang out in different places throughout the Americas. Both types of vultures prefer open spaces such as grasslands, deserts, and **scrublands** where they can easily **forage** for food.

What's for lunch?

Their bald heads help vultures stay clean when they stick their beaks into the **carcass** of a dead, rotting animal to eat. Yuck! Eating a rotting animal may sound nasty, but it's actually really helpful. It keeps the **environment** clean by getting rid of dead animals that may also be carrying diseases. The strong acid in vultures' stomachs allows them to digest this yucky kind of food.

The wow factor!

Unlike many other birds, vultures lay their eggs on the ground. The mother lays just one egg, though. Both the mother and father help feed the baby by **regurgitating** food from their own stomachs for the little one to enjoy. Eeww! How would you like to eat your mother's regurgitated breakfast?

How are they doing?

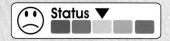

Conservation status:
Varies

Some species of vultures are stable, while others are threatened. In India, for example, vultures are dying because they eat dead farm animals that have medicines in their bodies that are harmful to vultures. The government of India has now made these medicines against the law, but they are still being used in other places. Vultures are also threatened by loss of **habitat** due to farming.

Dean's Journal...

"Vultures will never win a beauty contest. But they do play such an important role in the habitat by cleaning up dead animals. In southern Ethiopia, I found these two vultures cleaning up what was left of an antelope carcass. They didn't seem very interested in sharing, and that was just fine with me!"

— Dean Jacobs

Ww Wildebeest

Wildebeest
Scientific name:
Connochaetes taurinus
Scientists recognize 2 types of wildebeests: blue and black. Wildebeest is Dutch for "wild beast."

▲ This is a herd of wildebeests. They look a little like cows, but they are actually part of the antelope family.

This is a group of wildebeests. They stay together in large groups (herds) to help protect against predators.

Wildebeests love to eat grass. They will travel long distances for their food. How far do you travel for your food?

Where I Live On Our Planet
Wildebeests live in Africa, mostly in the Serengeti.

A B C D E F G H I J K L M N O P Q R S T U V **W** X Y Z

Big or small?

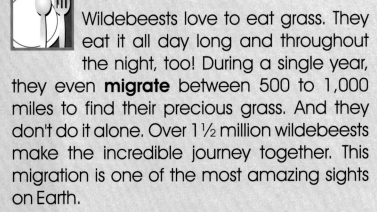

Wildebeests look a little bit like cows, but they are actually part of the antelope family. These three animals all have hooves that are divided into two toes. Can you imagine walking on two toes? Both male and female wildebeests can stand around 4½-feet tall and weigh up to 600 pounds.

Habitat:

As you can guess, wildebeests live on grassy plains and open woodlands where lots of grass can grow. They can be found only on the continent of Africa, mostly in the Serengeti National Park in Tanzania and the Masai Mara Game Reserve in Kenya.

What's for lunch?

Wildebeests love to eat grass. They eat it all day long and throughout the night, too! During a single year, they even **migrate** between 500 to 1,000 miles to find their precious grass. And they don't do it alone. Over 1 ½ million wildebeests make the incredible journey together. This migration is one of the most amazing sights on Earth.

The wow factor!

Scientists are studying the intelligence of wildebeests. They want to find out why wildebeests cross crocodile-infested rivers in one big swarm. Is it because they are in a **frenzy** to get to the grass on the other side? Or is it because they have figured out that it is safer to go across in a large group? Scientists also think wildebeests are smart because they take turns sleeping at night so they can stand guard against **predators**.

How are they doing?

Conservation status:
Stable

Because most wildebeests live in **national parks**, they are protected and their numbers are stable. **Drought** threatens wildebeests. However, the greater threat wildebeests face is the increase in the number of people who are farming and placing fences across migration routes.

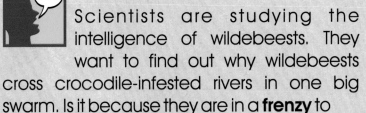

Dean's Journal...

"Viewing the wildebeest migration through the Serengeti in Africa was like watching an endless black stream weave its way around trees and large boulders. This would go on for what seemed like forever until the last wildebeest disappeared in a cloud of dust."

— Dean Jacobs

A B C D E F G H I J K L M N O P Q R S T U V W **X** Y Z

Xx

Write your animal's name here! ↑

You are the eXplorer. Now it's your turn! Create your own animal whose name starts with the letter "X".

Be the eXplorer and create an "X" animal!

Did you know that when a scientist discovers a new animal, he or she gets to name it?

Now it's your turn to be the explorer and scientist!

You create an animal whose name starts with the letter "X".

Put your animal's name at the top of this page and draw a picture of it here in the big box.

Be sure to tell about your new animal on the next page.

Have fun!

Your animal can be anything you want it to be. The only rule is that its name has to start with the letter "**X**".

Where does your animal live?

Color the areas on the map where your animal lives.

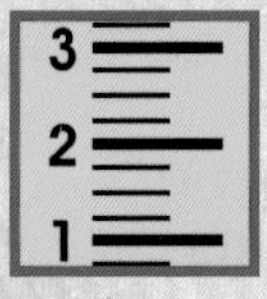

Big or small?

What is the size of your animal? What else is that size?

3
2
1

_____
_____
_____
_____
_____

Habitat

Where does your animal live? Where does it sleep and eat?

_____
_____
_____
_____
_____

What's for lunch?

What does your animal like to eat?

_____
_____
_____
_____
_____

The wow factor!

What is special about your animal?

_____
_____
_____
_____
_____

How are they doing?
Conservation status:

If your animal is safe from extinction, draw a happy face.
If your animal is not safe from extinction, draw a sad face.

Why is your animal safe or unsafe from extinction?

_____
_____
_____
_____
_____
_____

Tell a story about your animal or anything that you would like to share.

Your Journal...

_____
_____
_____
_____
_____
_____
_____
_____
_____
_____
_____
_____

Y y Yak

A
B
C
D
E
F
G
H
I
J
K
L
M
N
O
P
Q
R
S
T
U
V
W
X
Y
Z

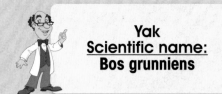

Yak
Scientific name:
Bos grunniens

▲ These are yaks. They are part of the herd this farmer cares for. What animal does a yak look like?

Yaks can live high in the mountains where it is very cold. Their long fur helps keep them warm in places like Nepal.

Here are the farmer's yaks getting a drink from a lake in Mongolia. Can you spot the farmer caring for the yaks?

Unlike deer, both male and female yaks have horns.

Where I Live On Our Planet

Red represents where yaks are found in Mongolia, Nepal, China, and India.

Big or small?

Yaks are closely related to cows. They share a similar shape and size, including a two-toed hoof. Female yaks weigh an average of 530 pounds, while males can weigh up to 1,000 pounds. A difference between cows and yaks is their coats. Yaks have a much thicker, two-layered coat.

Habitat:

Because yaks have a two-layered coat, they are well **adapted** to living in bitter cold climates. Most yaks today are **domesticated**, or kept by farmers. The few yaks left in the wild live on treeless **plateaus** and high mountains between 10,000 and 18,000 feet.

What's for lunch?

Even though most yaks are cared for by farmers, they will not eat grain like cows do. They prefer to graze on mountain grasslands in the summer. During the winter, they feed on shrubs when deep snow covers their precious grass.

The wow factor!

Did you know that yaks sweat just like people? The sweat of yaks is extra sticky. The stickiness helps keep the bottom layer of their coats matted to protect them from the bitter cold temperatures they live in. People sometimes use this sweat for medicine.

How are they doing?

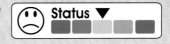

Conservation status:
Vulnerable

Yaks are very important farm animals in many parts of Asia. People use them for transportation, meat, and milk. Yak hair is used to make clothing. Some people even burn the dried **dung** as fuel.

There are about 12 million domesticated yaks in the world. Wild yaks, however, number only a few hundred and are very **vulnerable** to **extinction**. The biggest danger to wild yaks is hunting by people.

China and India have passed laws to protect them, but it is hard to **enforce** these laws in the huge, open spaces where the yaks live.

Dean's Journal...

"Standing next to a large white yak in the countryside of Mongolia, I was amazed how large he got and how long his hair was. Given how cold it was (-25 degrees Fahrenheit), I am sure he was happy to have such long hair. But it didn't make the fermented yak milk I had to drink taste any better."

— Dean Jacobs

Z z Zebra
(plains zebra)

Zebra
Scientific name:
Equus quagga
According to scientists, there are 3 species of zebras and several subspecies.

▲ These zebras look like they are wearing striped pajamas, but those stripes are really their natural coloring!

Where I Live On Our Planet
Plains zebras live in the red areas of Africa.

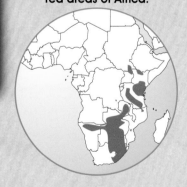

No two zebras' stripes are the same. Just like human fingerprints!

This is an adult zebra with a baby zebra. Male baby zebras are called colts. Female baby zebras are called foals. That is the same as horses!

Zebras look like horses but are not as tall. They stay together in groups for protection from predators.

Big or small?

Zebras are closely related to horses. You can tell this just by looking at them! Zebras stand around 4½-feet tall at their shoulders and weigh an average of 725 pounds. Horses come in many different sizes, including the size of the average zebra. Both zebras and horses have one toe on their hooves and slender, pointed ears that can turn in any direction.

Habitat:

Zebras live in many different **habitats** such as grasslands, **savannas**, woodlands, thorny **scrublands**, mountains, and coastal plains. Zebras are the **prey** of many **carnivores** that share their habitat, such as lions and hyenas. Thus, they find safety in numbers and like to hang out in large herds of up to thousands of zebras. That's a lot of stripes in one place!

What's for lunch?

Zebras graze on the grasses of Africa for at least half of their days. Sometimes it's hard to tell whether they are grazing or sleeping because they sleep standing up. They will only sleep, however, if they know other zebras are on guard to warn them of **predators**.

The wow factor!

Speaking of stripes, did you know the stripes of zebras are like their fingerprints? That's because no two zebras have exactly the same pattern.

Scientists are trying to figure out why zebras have stripes at all. Some think it's because the stripes make it harder for predators to tell one zebra from another. All those stripes make them look like one big animal, especially when they are running.

How are they doing?

Conservation status:

Plains zebras: Least Concern

As with most wild **species**, the biggest threat to zebras is their habitat being changed or destroyed by human activity. The biggest problem is that people, and their farm animals, are moving into areas where zebras live. Zebras are also hunted for their skins.

Dean's Journal...

"Watching a herd of zebras in the Serengeti in Africa is like going to a referee convention, black and white stripes all over and going in every direction possible. While lying in my tent at night, I heard zebras laughing in the distance. What a wonderful way to fall asleep."

— Dean Jacobs

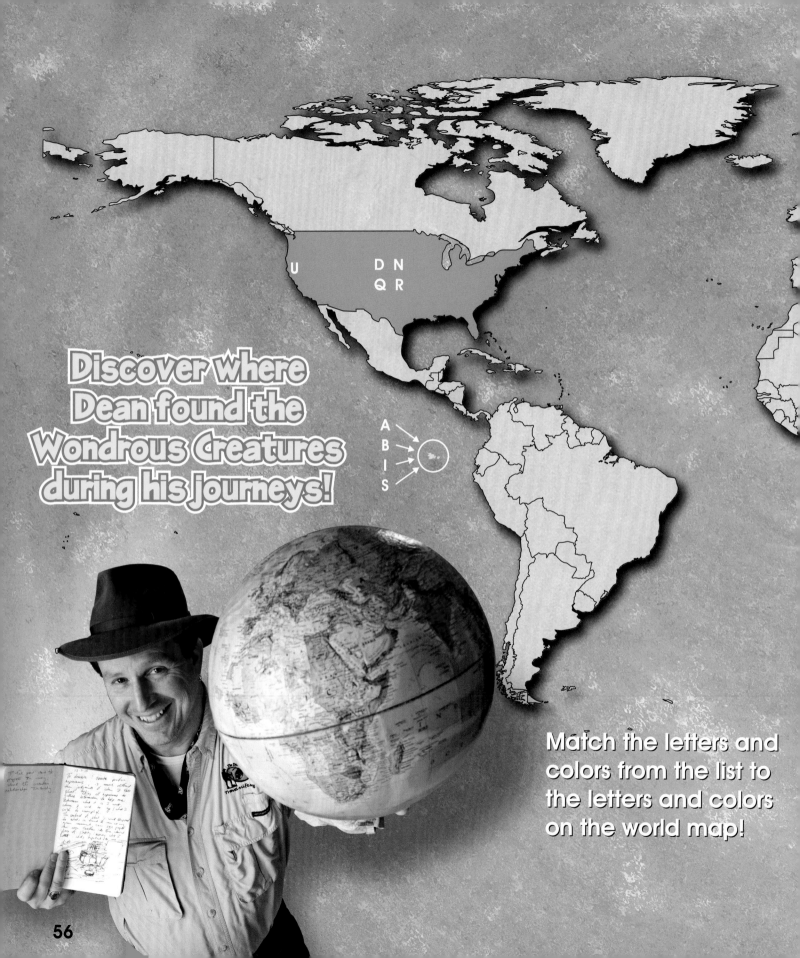

Discover where Dean found the Wondrous Creatures during his journeys!

U

D N
Q R

A
B
I
S

Match the letters and colors from the list to the letters and colors on the world map!

Ⓐ	Albatross	Galápagos Islands, Ecuador	Ⓝ	Newt	Nebraska, USA
Ⓑ	Blue-Footed Boobie	Galápagos Islands, Ecuador	Ⓞ	Orangutan	Indonesia
Ⓒ	Crocodile	Uganda (Africa)	Ⓟ	Panda	China
Ⓓ	Deer	Nebraska, USA	Ⓠ	Quail	Nebraska, USA
Ⓔ	Elephant	Tanzania, Uganda, Rwanda (Africa)	Ⓡ	Rabbit	Nebraska, USA
Ⓕ	Flamingo	Kenya (Africa)	Ⓢ	Seal	Galápagos Islands, Ecuador
Ⓖ	Gorilla	Rwanda (Africa)	Ⓣ	Tasmanian Devil	Tasmania, Australia
Ⓗ	Hippopotamus	Uganda (Africa)	Ⓤ	Urchin	Oregon, USA
Ⓘ	Iguana	Galápagos Islands, Ecuador	Ⓥ	Vulture	Ethiopia (Africa)
Ⓙ	Jackal	Namibia (Africa)	Ⓦ	Wildebeest	Tanzania (Africa)
Ⓚ	Koala	Australia	Ⓧ	_____	_____
Ⓛ	Leopard	Tanzania (Africa)	Ⓨ	Yak	Mongolia, Nepal
Ⓜ	Monkey	Rwanda (Africa)	Ⓩ	Zebra	Tanzania, Rwanda (Africa)

To find the meaning of a word, look in the  **Glossary**

Adaptable: to change to fit a new situation

Algae: a simple plantlike organism that mostly grows in water

Altitude: the upward distance of an object above a given level (as sea level)

Ambush: when the attacker hides from its prey and surprises it

Camouflage: hiding something by covering it up or changing the way it looks

Cancer: a tumor or growth that spreads to other parts of the body and often causes death

Carcass: a dead body

Carnivore: a meat eater

Characteristic: something that makes it recognizable

Crustacean: an animal that has a hard shell, lives in water, has hinged legs and bodies

Decline: to become less

Devastate: to ruin something

Digest: to change food into a simpler form that can be used by the body

Domesticated: to live with humans and serve their purposes

Dormant: when growth slows or stops

Drought: a long period of dry weather

Dung: fecal matter of an animal (commonly known as poo)

Ecosystem: a community of living things interacting with their environment under natural conditions

Enforce: to make sure something happens

Environment: everything that surrounds all living things and affects the growth, development, and survival of living things

Evolve: to change into something else

Extinct: no longer exist

Extinction: the process of disappearing from the planet

Ferocious: intense and scary

Feisty: full of energy to be active

Forage: a search for food

Frenzy: a wild burst of energy and activity

Freshwater: water with a low amount of salt

Habitat: the place where a plant or animal naturally or normally lives

Hatchling: a newly hatched animal

Herbivore: a plant-eating animal

Some of the words in your book might be new to you. To find out what they mean, just look for them here. First, find the **bold, thick word** on the animal pages. Then, find the meaning of the word here in the **glossary!**

Humongous: really big

Illegally: against the law

Kelp: a plant with large leaves that lives in the sea

Larvae: the immature, wingless, feeding stage of an insect that undergoes complete metamorphosis or change

Legally: permitted by law

Mammal: a warm-blooded vertebrate that includes human beings and all other animals that feed milk to their young and have hair or fur

Marsupials: a mammal that has a pouch on the front side of the female for carrying and feeding its young

Migrate: to move from one area to another, usually on a regular schedule for feeding or breeding

National Park: an area of land with special importance that is set aside and taken care of by a national government

Nocturnal: to be active at night

Omnivore: feeds on both animals and plants

Opposable: the thumb on a hand that can be moved and has the ability to touch each of the other fingers; this allows the animals to grasp items

Plateau: an elevated, generally level, large area of land

Poaching: to hunt or fish illegally

Pollution: waste made by humans that spoils the environment

Population: a group of organisms living in a certain habitat

Predator: an animal that lives by eating other animals

Prey: an animal hunted by another animal for food

Refuge: a place that provides protection

Regurgitate: bring the contents of the stomach back up into the mouth

Reptile: cold-blooded, air-breathing vertebrate that usually lays eggs and has skin covered with scales

Resilient: the ability to adjust to change

Rodent: a small mammal that has sharp front teeth for gnawing

Savanna: open grassland with scattered trees

Scrublands: land covered with small or stunted shrubs or trees

Species: a group of living things that shares common characteristics

Suburb: a smaller town on the outer edge of a city

Toxic: something that contains a poisonous substance

Vegetarian: a plant eater

Vulnerable: able to be attacked or hurt

Bibliography

1. **International Union for Conservation of Nature and Natural Resources**
   www.iucnredlist.org

2. **University of Michigan Animal Diversity Web**
   http://animaldiversity.ummz.umich.edu/site/index.html

3. **San Diego Zoo**
   http://kids.sandiegozoo.org

4. **National Geographic for Kids**
   http://kids.nationalgeographic.com/kids

5. **African Wildlife Foundation**
   www.awf.org

6. **Kiwi Conservation Club**
   www.kcc.org.nz

7. **Sea World Adventure Parks**
   www.seaworld.org

The Authors

Dean Jacobs

Dean Jacobs is a Nebraska native. Growing up in the Midwest gave him an appreciation for the simple things in life. He graduated from Wayne State College in Nebraska, earning a degree in Biology.

Dean's career began as the Assistant to the President of Wayne State College. Eventually his path led to Pfizer Pharmaceuticals where he was employed in sales/marketing for 10 years.

After a great deal of soul-searching, Dean left the security of corporate America and decided to pursue other dreams. This was the beginning of a process that led to a traveling adventure spanning nearly four years and covering over 50 countries. This included a seven-month field assignment for the Dian Fossey Gorilla Fund International in Rwanda, Africa.

When Dean isn't exploring, he travels across the U.S. and abroad presenting programs at schools, leading writing workshops, and giving keynotes to organizations about exploring the world and fulfilling dreams.

Amy Tharp

Amy Tharp has spent her 24-year career in education inspiring children to read and to write. Her master's program at Regis University in Denver, Colorado instilled the love of writing for Amy and she has never looked back. She brings her enthusiasm for writing to children as a classroom teacher, literacy specialist, and instructional coach.

In recent years, she has combined literacy skills with technology to guide students in following Dean Jacobs in his travels around the world. Amy has incorporated Dean's work into many aspects of her classroom.

Due to the success of these projects, Amy and Dean have presented at state, national, and international technology and literacy conferences. Amy is currently an instructional coach and first grade teacher in Littleton, Colorado.

Photo: Steve Schuenke